Property and Conveyancing Library

DILAPIDATIONS

THE MODERN LAW AND PRACTICE

AUSTRALIA
Law Book Co.
Sydney

CANADA and USA
Carswell
Toronto

NEW ZEALAND
Brookers
Auckland

SINGAPORE and MALAYSIA
Sweet & Maxwell Asia
Singapore and Kuala Lumpur

PROPERTY AND CONVEYANCING LIBRARY

DILAPIDATIONS

THE MODERN LAW AND PRACTICE

FIRST SUPPLEMENT TO THE

THIRD EDITION

by

Nicholas Dowding, Q.C., M.A. (Cantab.)

and

Kirk Reynolds, Q.C., M.A., (Cantab.), Hons. RICS

LONDON
SWEET & MAXWELL
2008

Published in 2008 by
Sweet & Maxwell Limited of
100 Avenue Road
London
NW3 3PF
www.sweetandmaxwell.thomson.com

Typeset by YHT Ltd, London
Printed and bound in Great Britain by Ashford Colour Press Ltd, Gosport

No natural forests were destroyed to make this product,
only farmed timber was used and replanted

A C.I.P. Catalogue record for this book is available from the British Library

ISBN 9780421921504

ACKNOWLEDGEMENTS

The Pre-Action Protocol for Claims for Damages in Relation to the Physical State of Commercial Property at the End of a Lease reproduced herein is the copyright of the Property Litigation Association and is reproduced with their kind permission.

HOW TO USE THIS SUPPLEMENT

This supplement generally follows the structure of the main work. Those chapters which have been updated are set out in the same order in which they appear in the main work, and are updated by reference to the relevant paragraph number.

PREFACE

The Third Edition of this work appeared in 2004, and was intended to state the law as of July 30, 2004. Since then there have been a number of important developments in the law and practice of dilapidations. There are two that can perhaps be singled out: the decision of the Court of Appeal in *Latimer v Carney* [2006] 3 E.G.L.R. 13, which (amongst other things) clarifies the law in relation to the extent to which claims for damages for breach of a covenant to decorate fall within s. 18(1) of the Landlord and Tenant Act 1927, and the publication by the Property Litigation Association of a new edition of its excellent pre-action Protocol. These and a number of other significant developments in the law of dilapidations have justified the publication of this supplement, which is intended to be followed in due course by a new Fourth Edition of the main work.

Chapter 34 (Tax Aspects of Dilapidations) has not been updated.

As always, we record our debt to our many friends and colleagues in the legal and surveying professions, whose wisdom and practical experience has been—and continues to be—invaluable. We are particularly grateful on this occasion to Alison Oakes, Barrister, of Landmark Chambers, who has ably assisted us in the preparation of this Supplement and for whose meticulous hard work we are indebted.

Nicholas Dowding Q.C
Kirk Reynolds Q.C.
Falcon Chambers
Falcon Court
London EC4Y 1AA

PREFACE

CONTENTS

SUPPLEMENTARY TABLE OF CASES

(References are to paragraph numbers)

SUPPLEMENTARY TABLE OF STATUTES

(References are to paragraph numbers)

SUPPLEMENTARY TABLE OF STATUTORY INSTRUMENTS

(References are to paragraph numbers)

CHAPTER 1

THE EXISTENCE OF THE OBLIGATION

COLLATERAL CONTRACTS

In *Business Environment Bow Lane v Deanwater Estates* [2007] L. & T. R. **1–03**
185 it was held at first instance that assurances by the landlord, prior to the
entry into a lease, that no terminal schedule of dilapidations would be served
on the tenant at the end of the lease were not intended to be overridden by a
clause in the lease. The Court of Appeal allowed the landlord's appeal on
the ground that the evidence did not show that the parties intended to make
any contract other than that arising from the grant of the lease.

IMPLIED TERMS

Terms implied in fact

B. P. Refinery (Westernport) v Shire of Hastings was followed in *Janet* **1–07**
Reger International v Tiree [2006] 3 E.G.L.R. 131, in which Mr Terence
Mowschenson QC (sitting as a deputy judge of the Chancery Division)
refused to imply an obligation upon the landlord to put the structure in
good condition on the basis that to do so would be to transfer work falling
within the tenant's repairing covenant to the landlord.

ESTOPPEL

See also *Business Environment Bow Lane v Deanwater Estates* [2007] L. & T. **1–13**
R. 185, considered in para. 1–03 above.

CHAPTER 3

WHO CAN SUE AND BE SUED

NEW TENANCIES

The liability of the original landlord under a new tenancy

First Penthouse Ltd v Channel Hotels & Properties (UK) Ltd is now also **3–22** reported at [2004] 1 E.G.L.R. 16 and [2004] L. & T. R. 27.

ASSIGNMENTS OF RIGHTS OF ACTION UNDER REPAIRING COVENANTS

Introductory

The general principle is that the assignee of a cause of action is in no better **3–34** position than his assignor. This may be relevant in a dilapidations context where (for example) the lease ends, the tenant vacates and the landlord then sells his interest to a third party, together with the benefit of his right of action against the outgoing tenant for damages for breach of the repairing covenants in the lease. In such a case, the price he obtains may well represent either the market value of the premises in repair or something very close to it. The tenant may argue that the effect of the sale is that the landlord/ assignor has suffered no loss and therefore that the assignee (being in no better position) is not entitled to substantial damages. In other words, what would otherwise have been a perfectly valid claim by the landlord/assignor has fallen into a legal 'black hole'. However, two recent cases show that the Courts are very reluctant to accept this sort of argument. In *Technotrade v Larkstore* [2006] 3 E.G.L.R. 5 the general principle was held to be that the assignee can recover the same damages (but no greater amount) as the assignor could have recovered, if there had been no assignment and if the land had not been transferred to the assignee. Rix LJ said at the outset of his judgment that the relevant cases demonstrate the court's striving to ensure that wrongdoers do not escape from their liabilities, by reference to the general principle that a person can only recover for his own loss, because of the happenstance that a cause of action lies in the hands of someone other than the person who suffered the loss. *Technotrade* was followed and applied in *Bizspace (NE) v Baird Corporatewear* [2007] 17 EG 174, in which the tenant sold its business and assets to a company which went into occupation of the premises pursuant to a licence, one of the terms of which was that the its occupation was to be subject to the same terms as the tenant's lease, and that the company would indemnify the tenant in respect of any breach of those terms. The tenant then assigned its rights to the landlord who brought proceedings against the company for terminal dilapidations. The correct principle was held to be that "the court should strive to ensure that a wrongdoer does not escape liability merely because the cause of action lies in the hands of someone other than the person who suffered the loss". The fact of the assignment did not therefore diminish the defendant's responsibility. Reference should also be made to *Catlin Estates v Carter Jonas* [2006] 2 E.G.L.R. 139 (in which it was held that a family company could recover damages against a building surveyor who had supervised a development notwithstanding that the completed building had been transferred at market value to the majority shareholder).

Whether the assignment is valid

3–35   See also *Massai Aviation Services and Another v A-G of the Bahamas* [2007] UKPC 12.

CHAPTER 4

THE CONSTRUCTION OF REPAIRING AND OTHER COVENANTS IMPOSING LIABILITY FOR DILAPIDATIONS

THE APPROACH OF THE COURTS TO THE INTERPRETATION OF REPAIRING AND OTHER COVENANTS RELATING TO THE CONDITION OF BUILDINGS

Words importing a meaning going beyond repair

(c) Obligations to keep in good or tenantable condition

See further H.H. Judge Coulson QC's summary of the relevant principles in   **4–27**
Carmel Southend v Strachan & Henshaw [2007] 35 EG 136.

Conditions precedent to the performance of landlord's covenants

Bluestorm Ltd v Portvale Holdings Ltd. is now also reported at [2004] 2   **4–33**
E.G.L.R. 38 and [2004] L. & T. R. 23.

CHAPTER 7

THE FIRST QUESTION: WHAT IS THE SUBJECT MATTER OF THE COVENANT?

THE DEMISED PREMISES

Difficulties and ambiguities

Footnotes 22 and 23: see further *Brian Maggs v Guy Marsh* [2006] E.W.C.A. **7–06**
Civ 1058, (2006) B.L.R. 396, and *Liaquat Ali v Robert Lane and Another*
[2007] 2 EG 126, where the circumstances in which regard may be had to the
parties' conduct when construing a contract are further considered.

Where the lease contains a covenant to contribute towards the costs of things used in common.

In *Delgable v Perinathan* [2006] 1 E.G.L.R. 78 the Court of Appeal relied **7–23**
upon a provision which required an underlessee of the first, second and third
floors to contribute a fair proposition of the costs of repairing "things the
use of which is common to the premises and other property adjoining or
near thereto" as pointing to the roof (which was nowhere expressly referred
to in the underlease) being excluded from the demise.

PARTICULAR PARTS OF THE DEMISED PREMISES AND PARTS OF THE BUILDING NOT INCLUDED IN THE DEMISE

Expressions commonly used to define the subject matter

(b) Main structure

In *Marlborough Park Services v Reeve* [2006] 2 E.G.L.R. 27 the question **7–34**
was whether, for the purposes of service charge recovery, the "main struc-
tures" of the building included the floor joists of the ceiling of the ground
floor flat and of the floor of the first floor. The Court of Appeal held that, as
a matter of ordinary language, the floor joists were part of the structure, and
there was nothing in the circumstances to require it to depart from the
statement to be found in *Irvine v Moran* (quoted in full in para. 732 of the
Main Text) that:

"the structure of the dwellinghouse consists of those elements of the overall dwellinghouse which gave it its essential appearance, stability and shape. The expression does not extend to the various ways in which the dwellinghouse will be fitted out, equipped, decorated and generally made to be habitable. I am not persuaded ... that one should limit the expression "the structure of the dwellinghouse" to those aspects of the dwellinghouse which are loadbearing in the sense that the expression is used by professional consulting engineers and the like; ... in order to be part of the structure of the dwellinghouse a particular element must be a material or significant element in the overall construction. To some extent, in every case there will be a degree of fact to be gone into to decide whether something is or is not part of the structure ... ."

Neuberger L.J. commented that this was "a good working definition to bear in mind, albeit not one to apply slavishly."

CHAPTER 8

THE SECOND QUESTION: IS THE SUBJECT MATTER OF THE COVENANT IN A DAMAGED OR DETERIORATED CONDITION?

THE REQUIREMENT OF DISREPAIR

In *Reger International v Tiree* [2006] 30 E.G. 102 (CS) the matters com- **8–01** plained of were caused by defective workmanship in relation to a damp-proof membrane forming part of the building's structure, and Mr Terence Mowschenson QC (sitting as a deputy judge of the Chancery Division) held that there was no relevant disrepair.

See also *Aljker v Collingwood Housing Association* [2007] 25 E.G. 184, considered below in relation to Chapter 20 (glass door panel made of ordinary annealed glass rather than safety glass not in disrepair for the purposes of the Defective Premises Act 1972).

CHAPTER 9

THE THIRD QUESTION: IS THE NATURE OF THE DAMAGE SUCH AS TO BRING THE CONDITION OF THE SUBJECT-MATTER BELOW THE STANDARD CONTEMPLATED BY THE REPAIRING COVENANT?

THE STANDARD OF REPAIR IMPOSED BY THE GENERAL COVENANT TO REPAIR

Substantial not perfect repair

See H.H. Judge Coulson QC's summary of the relevant principles in *Riverside Property Investments v Blackhawk Automotive* [2005] 1 E.G.L.R. 114 (TCC) and *Carmel Southend v Strachan & Henshaw* [2007] 35 E.G. 136 (considered below in relation to Chapter 12) .   **9–03**

The standard of repair under the general covenant

See H.H. Judge Coulson QC's summary of the relevant principles in *Riverside Property Investments v Blackhawk Automotive* [2005] 1 E.G.L.R. 114 (TCC) and *Carmel Southend v Strachan & Henshaw* [2007] 35 E.G. 136 (considered below in relation to Chapter 12).   **9–06**

The reasonably minded tenant

See H.H. Judge Coulson QC's summary of the relevant principles in *Riverside Property Investments v Blackhawk Automotive* [2005] 1 E.G.L.R. 114 (TCC) and *Carmel Southend v Strachan & Henshaw* [2007] 35 E.G. 136 (considered below in relation to Chapter 12).   **9–18**

COVENANTS TO KEEP THE PREMISES IN GOOD CONDITION

The relevant standard to which the subject matter must be kept

See further H.H. Judge Coulson QC's summary of the relevant principles in *Carmel Southend v Strachan & Henshaw* [2007] 35 E.G. 136.   **9–39**

Chapter 10

THE FOURTH QUESTION: WHAT WORK IS NECESSARY IN ORDER TO PUT THE SUBJECT-MATTER OF THE COVENANT BACK INTO THE CONTEMPLATED CONDITION?

WHERE THERE ARE SEVERAL POSSIBLE METHODS OF REMEDYING THE DEFECT

Different methods of repair

See H.H.J. Coulson QC's summary of the relevant principles in *Riverside Property Investments v Blackhawk Automotive* [2005] 1 E.G.L.R. 114 (TCC) and *Carmel Southend v Strachan & Henshaw* [2007] 35 E.G. 136 (considered below in relation to Chapter 12).   **10–04**

FUTILE WORK

Repetitive work as against a once and for all cure

In *Princes House and Another v Distinctive Clubs* (unreported decision of Mr. Jonathan Gaunt QC, sitting as a deputy judge of the Chancery Division, dated September 25, 2006) the landlord was required to use all reasonable endeavours to repair what was, in that case, a defective roof. The deputy judge held that, whilst the landlords had been entitled in the past to effect running or "patch" repairs, such a response was inadequate once it had become clear that the only adequate means of repair was to completely replace the roof. Given that the landlords were aware of the condition of the roof in 2001, their failure to carry out extensive repairs until 2004 was a breach of covenant.   **10–08**

See further H.H. Judge Coulson QC's summary of the relevant principles in *Carmel Southend v Strachan & Henshaw* [2007] 35 E.G. 136 (considered below in relation to Chapter 12).

CHAPTER 11

THE FIFTH QUESTION: IS THAT WORK NONETHELESS OF SUCH A NATURE THAT THE PARTIES DID NOT CONTEMPLATE IT WOULD BE THE LIABILITY OF THE COVENANTING PARTY?

EXPRESS WORDS

Covenants to keep in good condition

See further H.H. Judge Coulson QC's summary of the relevant principles in   **11–44**
Carmel Southend v Strachan & Henshaw [2007] 35 E.G. 136.

CHAPTER 12

THE APPLICATION OF THE REPAIRING COVENANT IN RELATION TO COMMONLY ENCOUNTERED DEFECTS

ROOFS

Where there are several available options

(a) Whether the lesser work complies with requisite standard of repair

A case going the other way on the facts is *Riverside Property Investments v* **12–08**
Blackhawk Automotive [2005] 1 E.G.L.R. 114 (TCC). There H.H. Judge
Coulson Q.C. found on the facts that the asbestos roof of the demised
premises, an industrial unit, had been capable of being brought up to the
requisite standard by works of repair falling short of total replacement. He
also found that the remedial works actually carried out by the tenant prior
to termination of the term had brought the roof up to the required standard.
He therefore dismissed the landlord's claim for damages based upon the
works actually carried out by the landlord, which consisted of removing the
newly-repaired roof and replacing it with an entirely new roof covering. The
judgment contains a detailed and instructive discussion of various practical
aspects relevant to the repair or replacement of an asbestos roof, including a
consideration of the landlord's argument (which the judge rejected) that to
attempt to repair such a roof would almost inevitably do more harm than
good, because further damage would be done in the course of replacing
defective asbestos sheets.

Much the same conclusion was reached by the same judge on similar facts
in *Carmel Southend v Strachan & Henshaw* [2007] 35 E.G. 136 (considered in
para. 12–09, below).

(b) The choice between methods

In the course of his judgment in *Riverside Property Investments Limited v* **12–09**
Blackhawk Automotive [2005] 1 E.G.L.R. 114 (TCC) Judge Coulson Q.C.
applied the principle set out in the text, saying (at para. 54):

"*Applicable principles of law*

[54] Although I have to decide whether there was a breach of this
covenant primarily by reference to the factual and expert evidence, it

seems to me that I must take into account the following particular principles of law in reaching my conclusion:

(i)   a covenant "well and substantially" to repair does not require the tenant to put the property into perfect repair (see *Proudfoot v Hart* (1890) 25 QB 42) or into a "pristine condition" (see *Commercial Union Life Assurance Co Ltd v Label Ink Ltd* [2001] L&TR 29);

(ii) the standard of repair is "that of an intending occupier of an industrial warehouse building, with modern construction, who judges repair reasonably by reference to his intended use of the premises": see *Commercial Union* above. In that case, Judge Rich QC, sitting as a deputy High Court judge in the Chancery Division, rejected the landlord's surveyor's evidence because "his complaints were against a standard of perfection: what a pristine building should look like, not what was required by covenant to keep what had been a pristine building in good and substantial repair";

(iii) the objective test referred to above must take into account the reasonably minded incoming tenant taking a lease of unit 4 on the same terms as the actual lease, including, in this case, a full repairing covenant: see para 9–06 of *Dowding and Reynolds on Dilapidations*;

(iv) if there is a dispute between replacement, on the one hand, and repair, on the other, replacement will be required only if repair is not reasonably or sensibly possible: *Ultraworth Ltd v General Accident Fire & Life Assurance Corporation plc* [2000] 2 E.G.L.R. 115 and *Dame Margaret Hungerford Charity Trustees v Beazeley* [1993] 2 E.G.L.R. 143. In the latter case, the Court of Appeal upheld the decision by the trial judge that, although everyone was agreed that a new roof was needed, the carrying out by the trustees of running repairs ensured that they complied with their repairing obligations in view of the age and character of the dwelling. I should add that, in this case, I do not consider that the words "where necessary" in the covenant either add or subtract from the principle identified above;

(v)   if there are two ways in which the covenant might properly be performed, the tenant is entitled to choose which method to utilise. Since the tenant is almost certainly going to choose the least expensive option, it cannot be criticised for so doing: see *Ultraworth* above. That position is not different to the situation concerning a claim for defects under a building contract where proper remedial works can be carried out in one of two ways. All other things being equal, the cheapest option will be appropriate: see the judgment of Judge Hicks QC in *George Fischer Holdings Ltd v Multi Design Consultants Ltd* (1968) 61 Con LR 85".

In *Carmel Southend v Strachan & Henshaw* [2007] 35 E.G. 136 the same judge upheld the tenant's contention that patch repairs would suffice to comply with the tenant's covenant to deliver up the premises "in good and substantial condition". The parties' surveyors had agreed that patch repairs were appropriate in the past, and the freeholder's surveyor had changed his position because of the freeholder's unilateral decision following pressure from the incoming tenant for a new roof to be provided. In the course of his judgment the judge set out what he considered to be the appropriate principles of law:

"8. *Standard of repair generally*

(a) A covenant "to keep in good and substantial repair" does not require the tenant to put the property into perfect repair (see *Proudfoot v Hart* (1890) 25 QBD 42) or pristine condition (see *Commercial Union Life Assurance Co Ltd v Label Ink Ltd* [2001] L. & T. R. 29).

(b) The standard of repair is that of an intending occupier "who judges repair reasonably by reference to his intended use of the premises": see *Commercial Union*. In that case, the judge criticised the landlord's surveyor for basing its complaints upon "what a pristine building should look like, not what was required by covenant to keep what had been a pristine building in good and substantial repair".

(c) An obligation to keep in good and substantial repair *and condition* is different and more extensive than an obligation merely to repair: see *Welsh v Greenwich London Borough Council* [2000] 49 E.G. 118. This may be wide enough to require the tenant to put the property into that condition even if it had never been in such condition before: see *Crédit Suisse v Beegas Nominees Ltd* [1994] 4 All E.R. 803. However, on that point, I accept [Counsel's] submission, on behalf of SH, that arguments about the difference, if any, made by the inclusion of the word "condition" in covenants of this type have tended to arise in circumstances where there is a challenge by the tenant to the scope of the works proposed or carried out by the landlord; where the tenant suggests that such works are so extensive that they have gone beyond mere repair. Here, that point does not arise directly because SH accepts that the overcladding was a repair option open to Carmel.

9. *Repair alternatives*

(a) If there is more than one possible method of repair, each of which would comply with the required standard, the choice is for the tenant to make (see para. 10–05 of *Dilapidations: The Modern Law and Practice* by Dowding and Reynolds (3rd ed.) 2004) and if there is a cost differential, the measure of damages at common law is based upon the less expensive option: see para. 29–12 of *Dowding and Reynolds*.

(b) Often, the dispute, such as the one in the present case, is between, on the one hand, a replacement option and, on the other, a repair option. In such circumstances, replacement will be required only if repair is not reasonably or sensibly possible: see *Ultraworth Ltd v General Accident Fire & Life Assurance Corporation plc* [2002] 2 E.G.L.R. 115 and *Dame Margaret Hungerford Charity Trustees v Beazeley* [1993] 2 E.G.L.R. 143. In the latter case, the Court of Appeal agreed with the trial judge that, although a new roof was required, the carrying out by the trustees of running repairs during the tenancy was enough to demonstrate compliance with their obligations, particularly given the age and character of the property in question.

(c) A tenant cannot rely upon its own breaches of covenant in order to lower the standard of repair. As Robert Walker J, as he then was, put it in *Ladbroke Hotels Ltd v Sandhu* (1996) 72 P. & C. R. 498 at p504:

"If a tenant disregards his repairing obligations and, as a result, the premises become run-down and commercially unattractive, it hardly lies in the tenant's mouth to rely on that fact as lowering the standard of repair required under the tenant's repairing covenant."

10. *Futility*

(a) There will be cases where, on the facts, the repairing covenant will require works that not only effect a repair but that also achieve the object of rendering continual repair work in the future unnecessary: see *Stent v Monmouth District Council* (1987) 54 P. & C. R. 193.

(b) In *Elmcroft Developments Ltd v Tankersley–Sawyer* [1984] 1 E.G.L.R. 47 (Court of Appeal), Ackner LJ, as he then was, said, at p49B–C:

"The patching work would have to go on and on and on, because, as the plaster absorbed (as it would) the rising damp, it would have to be renewed, and the cost to the appellants in constantly being involved with this sort of work, one would have thought, would have outweighed easily the cost in doing the job properly. I have no hesitation in rejecting the submission that the appellants' obligation was repetitively to carry out futile work instead in doing the job properly once and for all".

(c) I again accept [Counsel's] submission that both these cases, and other similar authorities relied upon by [opposing Counsel] were based upon findings of fact rather than general statements of principle.

11. *Incoming tenant*

    (a) The standard of repair must also take into account the reason-ably–minded incoming tenant taking a lease on the same terms as the actual lease, including, as in this case, a full repairing covenant: see para. 9–06 of *Dowding and Reynolds*.

    (b) In considering this aspect of the dispute, the court may have regard to the actual stance taken by the actual incoming tenant: see *Latimer v Carney* [2006] E.W.C.A. Civ 1417, and *Beegas*. However, the standard of repair is an objective one, which does not depend upon what, in the particular circumstances at the relevant time, an incoming tenant would accept: see para 9–18 of *Dowding and Reynolds*".

DAMP

Rising Damp

(b) Absence of a damp-proofing system

In *R (on the application of Sinclair Gardens Investments (Kensington) v Lands Tribunal* [2006] 3 All E.R. 650, [2006] 1 E.G.L.R 7, Neuberger L.J. emphasised that whether or not the installation of a damp proof course is required by a repairing covenant is "fact-sensitive and nuanced". In that case, after considering the reported decisions referred to in this paragraph, the Court of Appeal declined to interfere with the Land Tribunal's decision that the installation of a damp proof course was not repair within the meaning of the landlord's covenant. **12–28**

CHAPTER 18

DESTRUCTION OF THE SUBJECT MATTER

OBLIGATION NOT TO DESTROY

A question of construction

British Glass Manufacturers Confederation v Sheffield University is now also **18–03**
reported at [2004] 1 E.G.L.R. 40 and [2004] L. & T. R. 14.

Relevant considerations

British Glass Manufacturers Confederation v Sheffield University is now also **18–07**
reported at [2004] 1 E.G.L.R. 40 and [2004] L. & T. R. 14.

CHAPTER 18

DISTRIBUTION OF THE SUBJECT MATTER

CHAPTER 19

THE LANDLORD'S IMPLIED OBLIGATIONS TO TOWARDS THE TENANT AT COMMON LAW

INTRODUCTORY

The general principle

See also *Reger International v Tiree* [2006] 30 E.G. 102 (CS), in which Mr   **19–02**
Terence Mowschenson QC (sitting as a deputy judge of the Chancery
Division) refused to imply an obligation upon the landlord to put the
structure in good condition on the basis that to do so would be to transfer
work falling within the tenant's repairing covenant to the landlord.

CHAPTER 20

THE LANDLORD'S IMPLIED OBLIGATIONS TO TOWARDS THE TENANT UNDER STATUTE

SECTION 11 OF THE LANDLORD AND TENANT ACT 1985: SHORT LEASES OF DWELLING-HOUSES

Terms implied in the case of tenancies entered into before January 15, 1989

(b) the structure and exterior of the dwelling house

Niazi Services Ltd v Van der Loo is now also reported at [2004] 1 E.G.L.R. 62.   **20–26**

Further terms implied into tenancies granted on or after January 15, 1989

Niazi Services Ltd v Van der Loo is now also reported at [2004] 1 E.G.L.R. 62.   **20–32**

SECTION 4 OF THE DEFECTIVE PREMISES ACT 1972

When the duty arises

In *Aljker v Collingwood Housing Association* [2007] 25 E.G. 184 the lease   **20–54**
contained a landlord's repairing covenant requiring the landlord to keep the
property in good condition and to repair and maintain the structure and
interior of the building. The front door to the property contained a glass
panel made of ordinary annealed glass rather than safety glass. The tenant
accidentally put her hand through the window and injured herself. At first
instance the judge held that the annealed glass was a "relevant defect"
within the meaning of section 4 of the Defective Premises Act 1972. The
Court of Appeal allowed the landlord's appeal on the basis that the door
was not in disrepair and the section 4 duty extends no further than the
covenant to maintain and repair owed by the landlord in any particular
case. It is not a warranty that premises are reasonably safe where there is no
disrepair.

CHAPTER 22

CONSIDERATIONS AFFECTING THE PERFORMANCE OF THE LANDLORD'S OBLIGATIONS TO REPAIR

WHEN THE LANDLORD'S OBLIGATION MUST BE PERFORMED

Sufficiency of notice

In *Princes House and Another v Distinctive Clubs* [2007] 27 E.G. 304 there   **22–06**
was an express term requiring the tenant to give notice to the landlord of
disrepair. The Court of Appeal held that the landlord could not rely upon
the clause to exonerate itself from liability because it had informed the
tenants that it intended to carry out the repairs and so had waived the
requirement for notice.

THE LANDLORD'S RIGHTS OF ENTRY TO CARRY OUT WORKS

The general principle where no express right of entry is reserved

Akram v Adam is now also reported at [2007] 1 W.L.R. 2762 and [2005] 1 All   **22–28**
E.R. 741.

Rights of entry under statute

(b) Regulated tenancies under the Rent Act 1977

Akram v Adam (wrongly referred to in the text as *Akram v Smee*) is now also   **22–37**
reported at [2007] 1 W.L.R. 2762 and [2005] 1 All E.R. 741.

CHAPTER 25

FIXTURES

Tenant's fixtures and landlord's fixtures

In *Indiana Investments v Taylor* [2004] 3 E.G.L.R. 63 Judge Roger Cooke **25–19** relied upon the corresponding and following paragraphs in the 2nd edition of the main work as being "a convenient summary of known authority" albeit that "the learned authors are still alive and in practice".

CHAPTER 27

FORFEITURE

THE SECTION 146 NOTICE

Service of the notice

Beanby Estates v Egg Stores (Stamford Hill) Ltd is now also reported at   **27–25**
[2004] 3 All E.R. 184.

CHAPTER 28

OTHER REMEDIES DURING THE TERM

DAMAGES DURING THE TERM

Section 18(1) of the Landlord and Tenant Act 1927

In *Irontrain Investments v Salim Ansari* (unreported, February 24 2005, **28–20** Central London County Court) H.H. Judge Mackie Q.C. held that where a landlord was claiming damages for breach of a repairing obligation in his capacity as lessee, and not in his capacity as landlord, section 18(1) of the Landlord and Tenant Act 1927 does not apply. On appeal the Court of Appeal ([2005] E.W.C.A. Civ 1681) did not consider the point because they found that the defendant tenant was in any event liable in negligence.

CHAPTER 29

DAMAGES AT THE END OF THE TERM (1): CLAIMS TO WHICH SECTION 18(1) OF THE LANDLORD AND TENANT ACT 1927 APPLIES

THE MEASURE OF DAMAGES AT COMMON LAW

The cost of the works

The doubt expressed by the Authors as to whether *Joyner v Weeks* would be decided the same way today derives support from obiter dicta of Arden L.J. in *Latimer v Carney* [2006] 3 E.G.L.R. 13. She said (at para 60):   **29–08**

> "It may be that the Courts would not apply the common law measure of damages in all cases today. I would accept the argument of counsel ... that, if the common law measure alone were relevant to a landlord's claim, the courts today might in an appropriate case adopt the measure of damages in section 18(1) in preference to that which has previously been held to be the measure at common law (see *Ruxley v Forsyth*)".

THE FIRST LIMB OF SECTION 18(1) OF THE LANDLORD AND TENANT ACT 1927

Introductory

See para. 31–13, below.   **29–19**

Where the premises have potential for redevelopment or refurbishment

In *Latimer v Carney* [2006] 3 E.G.L.R. 13 Arden L.J. referred to the text and quoted that part in which the view is expressed that "depending on the facts, the diminution in value of the reversion might well be limited to the cost of those repairs which would survive the refurbishment". She then set out the quotation which appears in the text from Mr Colin Reese Q.C. in *Firle Investments Limited v Datapoint International Limited*, and pointed out that there was a difference between the two propositions, because Mr Reese "had made the proposition far firmer and more absolute than Dowding and Reynolds". Nonetheless she approved the Authors' formulation, stating that: **29–41**

"I consider that the judge's reformulation must be treated as not departing from Dowding and Reynolds. On this basis, what Mr Colin Reese holds is that it is *likely* that there is no diminution in value when repair works are superseded by works of refurbishment that would be undertaken by the purchaser. Later passages in the judge's judgment support a more nuanced approach ...".

Where the premises are sub-let on the relevant date

(b) Where the premises are occupied by sub-tenants entitled to the protection of Part II of the Landlord and Tenant Act 1954

29–44   These passages were approved in *Lyndendown v Vitamol* [2007] E.W.C.A. Civ 826; [2007] 29 E.G. 142 (CS). In that case the tenant sub-let the premises with the permission of the reversioner. The sub-lease contained covenants by the sub-lessee to observe and perform the covenants in the headlease. Prior to the granting of the sub-lease the tenant's parent company gave an undertaking in a side letter that it would be responsible for any repairs other than the obligation to keep the property wind and watertight. At the expiry of the headlease the sub-lessee remained in occupation under Part II of the Landlord and Tenant Act 1954. The reversioner sued the headtenant for breach of the repair covenants. It was common ground that, absent the existence of the side letter, there would be little or no diminution in the value of the reversion by reason of the breach of the repairing covenants. The judge at first instance held that the side letter did not alter the value of the reversion. The Court of Appeal, citing the views expressed on page 668 of the text, dismissed an appeal by the reversioner on the footing that the judge was entitled to reach his conclusion on the basis of the expert evidence before him.

The effect of failure to adduce valuation evidence as to the diminution in the value of the reversion

29–62   The decision in *Crewe* was applied in *Latimer v Carney* [2006] 3 E.G.L.R. 13. In that case the judge at first instance dismissed the landlord's claim on the basis that there had been no evidence of the cost of most of the actual works done (although the works set out in the schedule of dilapidations were accompanied by prices estimated by the landlord's building surveyor) and there were no formal valuations for the purposes of s.18(1). Allowing the appeal, the Court of Appeal awarded the landlord the full cost of repairing the roof (where evidence of the actual cost had been led) and the estimated cost of the other works, but subject to a discount of 60%, because, in all the circumstances of that case, the discount ought to be generous. Stating that the landlords had "themselves to blame for failing to foresee that the court would not have the raw material from which more precisely to draw inferences and that perhaps they thought they would be able to take a short cut", Arden L.J. said that, if that was the case "it is worth recalling the advice given" in this paragraph of the text. Arden L.J. then quoted the closing sentence of the paragraph.

CHAPTER 31

DAMAGES AT THE END OF THE TERM (2): CLAIMS TO WHICH SECTION 18(1) OF THE LANDLORD AND TENANT ACT 1927 DOES NOT APPLY

THE COMMON LAW MEASURE OF DAMAGES FOR BREACH OF AN OBLIGATION TO CARRY OUT WORKS

Cost of the works or diminution in value

Where a publishing company's archive of historic aviation material had been damaged by flooding and the company intended to reinstate the archive and it was reasonable to do so, the Court of Appeal held that the cost of reinstatement was the correct measure of damages: *Aerospace Publishing v Thames Water Utilities* [2007] EWCA Civ 3.   **31–03**

DAMAGES FOR BREACH OF COVENANT TO DECORATE

The measure of damages

The distinction suggested in the text does not seem to have been drawn in *Latimer v Carney* [2006] 3 E.G.L.R. 13, where the Court of Appeal cited with apparent approval the trial judge's observation that "a covenant to decorate premises during or at the end of the lease is in substance a species of repairing covenant". Arden L.J. added: **31–13**

> "In all the circumstances I think that this court should treat a failure to repair the decorative state of the premises as a breach of covenant to repair for the purposes of the first limb of section 18(1) even if that failure also constitutes a breach of a covenant for periodic decoration in the same lease".

CHAPTER 32

THE TENANT'S REMEDIES FOR BREACH OF CONTRACT ON THE PART OF THE LANDLORD

DAMAGES

Where the tenant remains in occupation

(a) Inconvenience and discomfort

In *Earle v Charabambous* [2006] E.W.C.A. Civ 1090; (2007) H.L.R. 8, the **32–17** Court of Appeal held that, in assessing the appropriate award of damages in a residential case, distress and inconvenience were not freestanding heads of claim but were symptomatic of interference with the lessee's enjoyment of its asset. If the lessor's breach of covenant had the effect of depriving the lessee of that enjoyment for a significant period, a notional judgment of the resulting reduction in rental value was likely to be the most appropriate starting point of assessment of damages. The Court of Appeal rejected the argument that assessing damages by reference to a notional rent was not appropriate where the tenant occupied under a long lease rather than a periodic tenancy and the loss of value was temporary: *Wildtree Hotels v Harrow London Borough Council* [2000] 2 E.G.L.R. 5 was applied.

Service charges

In *Princes House and Another v Distinctive Clubs* (unreported decision of Mr **32–36** Jonathan Gaunt Q.C., sitting as a deputy judge of the Chancery Division, dated September 25, 2006) the landlord was obliged to use all reasonable endeavours to complete works that he covenanted to carry out, subject to the tenant paying service charge reasonably and properly incurred in, inter alia, carrying out the works. The service charge was capped for the first five years of the lease (up to December 24, 2003). The landlord was aware by 2001 that extensive repairs were required to the roof and proposed in a letter to the tenants in 2002 that the works would be carried out in 2003 (i.e. before the expiry of the cap), but in breach of covenant the works were not commenced until 2004. The deputy judge held that had the works been carried out in accordance with the terms of the lease, the tenants' service charge contribution would have been subject to the cap. He therefore awarded damages on the basis of the excess service charge paid over and above the cap.

CARRYING OUT THE WORKS

Availability of setoff

32–46   To the cases referred to in this paragraph must be added *Edlington Properties v J.H. Fenner & Co.* [2006] 1 W.L.R. 1583, in which the Court of Appeal held that (where the reversion has been transferred) a tenant cannot set-off, against rent falling due after the transfer, a claim for damages that it has arising out of a breach by its original landlord under the lease unless the lease specifically provides that it should have that right.

Exclusion of the right of set-off

32–47   In *Edlington Properties Limited v J.H. Fenner & Co Limited* [2006] 1 W.L.R. 1583 it was held (applying the *Connaught Restaurant* case) that the right of equitable set-off was not excluded by the stipulation that the rent should be paid "without deduction or abatement".

CHAPTER 33

THE RECOVERY OF FEES AND COSTS

COSTS INCURRED IN ASCERTAINING THE BREACH AND IN COMPLYING WITH FORMALITIES

Express provision in lease

In *Riverside Property Investments Limited v Blackhawk Automotive* [2005] 1 **33–07** E.G.L.R. 114 (TCC) H.H. Judge Coulson Q.C. set out the following two principles, one of which was relevant to the proper construction of clause 22(b) of the lease with which he was concerned (which allowed the landlord to recover "all proper costs and expenses (including solicitors' costs and surveyors' fees) incurred by the lessor in or incidental to the preparation and service of any notice or schedule relating to the dilapidations)", and the other of which was relevant to clause 22(c) (which allowed the landlord to recover "all proper costs and expenses incurred by the lessor in or in connection with the enforcement of any of the lessee's covenants and conditions herein contained"). The principles were:

"*Principles relevant to costs claims*

[81] Principle 1

In order to be recoverable under clause 22(b), the item of cost or expenditure must be incidental to the preparation and service of any notice or dilapidations schedule. If the reason why the item of cost or expense was incurred was unconnected with the preparation of a dilapidations schedule, such as the proposed early surrender of the lease, it does not seem to me that it can be recoverable under clause 22(b) of the lease.

[82] Principle 2

The costs and expenses recoverable under clause 22(c) are those incurred in connection with the enforcement of the repairing covenants. Accordingly, the work for which the cost or expense is claimed must be work that was connected to attempts by Riverside to compel Blackhawk to perform those covenants. That must mean, in practice, that the work related to the collection of information or advice that was then passed on to Blackhawk in an attempt to get it to comply with the

covenants. Thus, items of work that were performed on behalf of
Riverside that went, say, to the preparation of reports that were never
passed on to Blackhawk and about which it was therefore ignorant,
cannot be costs incurred in connection with the enforcement of the
covenant".

CHAPTER 34

TAX ASPECTS OF DILAPIDATIONS

This Chapter has not been up-dated in this Supplement.

Chapter 35

DILAPIDATIONS QUESTIONS ARISING IN RELATED FIELDS

OPTIONS TO RENEW AND TO DETERMINE LEASES

Degree of compliance required

The test formulated by H.H. Judge Rich Q.C. in *Commercial Union Life* **35–12**
Assurance Co Limited v Label Ink Limited, as noted in the text, has now been
disapproved by the Court of Appeal in *Fitzroy House Exmouth Street (No1)
Limited v The Financial Times Limited* [2006] 2 E.G.L.R. 13, in which a
tenant's break clause was conditional on it having "materially complied with
all its obligations under this lease down to the [termination] date". It was
held that the test of material compliance was objective, and that materiality
was to assessed by reference to the landlord's ability to relet or sell the
property without delay or additional expenditure. The Chancellor said in his
judgment that:

> "I can agree that the insertion of the word "material" must have been in
> order to mitigate the requirement for absolute compliance with all
> covenants at the relevant time then to be found in conventional break
> clauses. Other variations, now common, are "reasonable" and "sub-
> stantial". However, I cannot agree that it must have been the intention
> to modify the rule to the extent that it is reasonably fair to both
> landlord and tenant. The word "material" is susceptible to a number of
> nuances, but what is fair and reasonable between landlord and tenant is
> not one of them".

He went on to say:

> "Materiality must be assessed by reference to the ability of the landlord
> to relet or sell the property without delay or additional expenditure.
> Where the provision is absolute, any breach will preclude an exercise of
> the break clause. However, I see no justification for attributing to the
> parties an intention that the insertion of the word "material" was
> intended to permit only those breaches that were trivial or trifling.
> Those words are of uncertain meaning also, and are not the words used
> by the parties.

Nor is it, in my view, of any assistance to consider whether the word "material" permits more or different breaches than the commonly used alternatives "substantial" or "reasonable". The words "substantial" and "material", depending upon the context, are interchangeable. The word "reasonable" connotes a different test. The issue here is whether, notwithstanding the breaches found by the judge, the tenant had nevertheless "materially complied" with its obligations".

Practical considerations for tenants

35–14   The quotation from Mellish L.J. in *Finch v Underwood* was explained, and the use made of it by H.H. Judge Rich Q.C. was disapproved, by the Court of Appeal in *Fitzroy House Exmouth Street (No.1) Limited v The Financial Times Limited* [2006] 2 E.G.L.R. 13. The Chancellor said [at 9]:

"I do not understand Mellish L.J. to be suggesting that the reasonable conduct of the tenant can justify a finding that a condition precedent has been satisfied notwithstanding the existence of a relevant breach of covenant. Rather, he is pointing out that, in the circumstances he postulates, the court would be likely to accept the evidence of the surveyor for the tenant to the effect that the covenant had been duly performed by the material time".

CHAPTER 36

DILAPIDATIONS CLAIMS IN PRACTICE

INTRODUCTORY

The Property Litigation Association's Pre-Action Protocol, originally issued **36–01** in Spring 2002, has now been brought out in a second edition, effective as from September 14, 2006. The new edition is entitled "Pre-Action Protocol for Claims for Damages in Relation to the Physical State of Commercial Property at the End of a Lease". It is re-printed, with the kind permission of the Property Litigation Association, which owns the copyright, at the end of this Supplement, where it replaces Appendix Three.

MATTERS TO BE TAKEN INTO ACCOUNT BY THE LANDLORD WHEN CONSIDERING MAKING A CLAIM FOR DILAPIDATIONS

Deciding whether to bring a claim

Although, at the time of writing this Supplement the PLA's Pre-Action **36–10** Protocol has not yet been formally adopted, the first edition has been endorsed by the Royal Institution of Chartered Surveyors in its Dilapidations Guidance Note (4th Edn) which states that:

> "Practitioners are encouraged to use it as a guide to good practice when addressing a terminal claim for dilapidations and should direct their clients' attention to it".

Since publication, the PLA Protocol has been subject to review and consultation, receiving comment from the Department of Constitutional Affairs, as well as from practitioners. A new edition of the PLA Protocol is effective from September 14 2006, and is reprinted at the end of this Supplement. The changes as between the two editions of the PLA Protocol are usefully summarised in an article by Jacqui Joyce and Keith Conway, "A new way of resolving differences" in the Estates Gazette (September 16, 2006). Those changes are also noted where appropriate in this Supplement. Save where noted otherwise, comments made in the text on the first edition of the PLA Protocol apply equally to the new edition.

THE PREPARATION OF THE SCHEDULE OF DILAPIDATIONS

Suggested form of Schedule under Protocols

36–22   The second edition of the PLA Protocol contains a revised suggested form of Schedule (Annex A), which is reprinted at the end of this Supplement. The original version has been shortened in the current edition, now identifying the landlord's case as to (a) the relevant clause, (b) the breach complained of, (c) the remedial works required and (d) costings. Para. 5.2 of the Protocol requires the tenant to respond to the Schedule, where appropriate, "in sufficient detail to enable the landlord to understand clearly the tenant's views on each item of claim". A number of columns are left blank for the tenant's use.

Claim where Protocols apply

36–25   The second edition of the PLA Protocol clarifies the difference between the Schedule and the Claim. So far as the Claim is concerned, the most notable difference between the first and current editions of the Protocol is the omission from the current edition of the obligation in the first edition to include a valuation for the purposes of s.18(1) of the Landlord and Tenant Act 1927 in all cases where the landlord does not intend to carry out the works. The previous requirement to provide such a valuation at such an early stage was felt by some practitioners to be potentially disproportionate in terms of time and cost. The requirement has now been put back (by para 4.8.5) to some time "prior to issuing proceedings". To counterbalance this, the current edition now provides (in para. 4.8.2) that the Claim "should not include any items likely to be superseded by works to be carried out by the landlord or items likely to be superseded by the landlord's intentions for the property", and (para. 4.8.3) that the Claim "must contain a written endorsement by the surveyor(s) preparing it that the overall figure claimed is a fair assessment of the landlord's loss". The new edition of the PLA Protocol also includes (in para. 10) a detailed set of requirements as to "formal diminution valuation and quantification of claim prior to issue of proceedings", illustrated by a flowchart at Annex C (printed at the end of this Supplement). These requirements distinguish, in particular, between the evidence of quantification which it is appropriate for the landlord to provide in a case where the landlord has carried out the work; where the landlord has carried out some of the work but not all of it; where the landlord has not carried out the work but intends to; and where the landlord does not intend to carry out the work. A tenant who relies on a defence on the basis of diminution is required to state his case for doing so and to provide a diminution valuation to the landlord.

FORMAL RESPONSE BY TENANT WHERE ONE OF THE PROTOCOLS APPLIES

There has been a small change in the recommended time for the tenant's **36–27** response as between the two editions of the PLA's Protocol, that time now being 56 days rather than two months. The tenant must respond "using the Schedule provided by the landlord". A new feature is that the tenant is now required (by para. 5.3) to state whether he considers that any items in the Claim "are likely to be superseded by works to be carried out by the landlord" and if so, to identify those items, give particulars of that on which he relies (e.g. correspondence or minutes of the landlord company), and state the items in the landlord's claim to which that contention is relevant.

NEGOTIATIONS AND COMPROMISE

Negotiations under the Property Litigation Association's Protocol

The new edition of the PLA Protocol supplements its previous recommen- **36–36** dation that the parties should negotiate with a lengthy new section (para. 8) on Alternative Dispute Resolution. Reference is now made to Mediation (see para. 38–08 of the Text) and Early Neutral Evaluation (see para. 38–09 of the Text).

CHAPTER 37

DILAPIDATIONS CLAIMS UNDER THE CIVIL PROCEDURE RULES

INTRODUCTORY

Position in dilapidations cases

The Property Litigation Association has brought out a new edition of its **37–04** Pre-Action Protocol (entitled "Pre-Action Protocol for Claims for Damages in Relation to the Physical State of Commercial Property at the End of a Lease") effective as from September 14 2006. It is re-printed, with the kind permission of the Property Litigation Association, which owns the copyright, at the end of this Supplement, where it replaces Appendix Three, and it is considered in the Supplement to Chapter 36, above.

JURISDICTION

The Technology and Construction Court

A new Technology and Construction Court Guide was published with effect **37–06** from October 3, 2005.

PRE-ACTION PROTOCOL FOR CLAIMS FOR DAMAGES IN RELATION TO THE PHYSICAL STATE OF COMMERCIAL PROPERTY AT THE END OF A LEASE (THE "DILAPIDATIONS PROTOCOL")

Property Litigation Association
14 September 2006

1. Introduction

1.1   This protocol applies to commercial property situate in England and Wales. There is a separate Pre-Action Protocol for Housing Disrepair cases.

1.2   This protocol relates to claims for damages for dilapidations against tenants at the expiry of the lease. These are generally referred to as terminal dilapidations claims.

1.3   It is not the purpose of this protocol to define "dilapidations", "repair", "reinstatement" or "redecoration". The work to the property that may be required will depend on the contractual terms of the lease and any other licences or other relevant documents. However, as a guide:

    1.3.1   "dilapidations" might be said to be a claim for all breaches of covenant or obligation relating to the physical state of a demised property at the end of the lease, and usually includes items of repair, redecoration and reinstatement.

    1.3.2   "repair" might be said to be a reference to a state of disrepair in a property, where there is a legal liability to remedy, or undertake, work to rectify it;

    1.3.3   "reinstatement" might be said to be a reference to returning a property to its former state prior to carrying out works of alteration, where there is a legal liability to remedy, or undertake, that work;

    1.3.4   "redecoration" might be said to be a reference to a state of general finish or appearance of the property as required by the lease, where there is a legal liability to remedy, or undertake, that work.

    1.3.5   The tenant may also be required to carry out other works for example, renewal, replacement and maintenance. This is not an exhaustive list.

1.4   This protocol is not intended to be an exhaustive or mandatory list of steps or procedures to be followed regardless of the circumstances. Those will be determined by the facts of each case. It is also not intended to be an explanation of the law. In deciding the exact steps and procedures to be adopted regard should also be had to the Overriding Objective as set out in CPR Part 1 and the Practice Direction—Protocols.

1.5 This protocol is intended to improve the pre-action communication between landlord and tenant by establishing a timetable for the exchange of information relevant to the dispute and by setting standards for the content of claims and, in particular, the conduct of pre-action negotiations.

1.6 Compliance with the protocol should enable both landlords and tenants to make an early informed judgment on the merits of their cases. The aim is to increase the number of pre-action settlements. If proceedings are commenced, the court will be able to treat the standards set out in this protocol as the normal reasonable approach to pre-action conduct when the court considers issues of costs and other sanctions under the CPR. When doing so, the court should be concerned with substantial compliance and not minor departures, e.g. failure by a short period to provide relevant information. In addition, minor departures should not exempt the "innocent" party from following the protocol. The court may also be invited to consider the effect of non-compliance on the other party when deciding whether to impose sanctions.

2. Overview of Protocol—General Aim

2.1 The objectives of this protocol are :-
  (a) to encourage the exchange of early and full information about the prospective legal claim;
  (b) to enable parties to avoid litigation by agreeing a settlement of the claim before the commencement of proceedings;
  (c) to support the efficient management of proceedings where litigation cannot be avoided.

2.2 A flow chart is attached at Annex C .

THE PROTOCOL

3. The Schedule

3.1 Generally, the landlord shall serve a schedule in the form attached at Annex A. It shall (a) indicate the breaches of the tenant's covenants or obligations which have not been remedied at the end of the lease, (b) state what in the opinion of the landlord or its surveyor is necessary to put the property into the physical state in accordance with the terms of the lease and any licences or other relevant documents, and (c) the landlord's costings (which may be based on its estimate or invoices if the works have been done).

3.2 Breaches should be separated into relevant categories eg repair, reinstatement, redecoration etc, and these should be listed separately in the schedule and should (where appropriate) identify any notices served by the landlord requiring reinstatement works to be undertaken.

3.3 The schedule shall be served within a reasonable time. A "reasonable time" will vary from case to case but generally will be not more than 56 days after the end of the lease.

3.4 The landlord may serve a schedule before the end of the lease. However, if it does so it should confirm at the end of the lease that the situation remains as in its earlier schedule or serve a further schedule within a reasonable time.

3.5 If possible the schedule should also be provided by way of computer disk or similar form to enable the tenant's comments to be incorporated in the one document.

4. The Claim

4.1 The schedule should set out what the landlord considers to be the breaches, the works required to be done to remedy those breaches and the landlord's costings (see 3.5 above). The claim should set out and substantiate the monetary sum the landlord is claiming as damages in respect of those breaches. This will include the items in the schedule and also any other items of loss it may wish to claim (see 4.6 below). The claim should be limited by the landlord's assessment of loss (see 4.8 below).

4.2 The claim should indicate clearly how it has been made up. The claim should be set out separately from the schedule but may be part of the same document.

4.3 If the claim is in a separate document from the schedule then this should also be served within the timescale for service of the schedule (see 3.3 above).

4.4 If the claim is based on the cost of works, it should be fully quantified and substantiated. For example, each item of expenditure should, where possible and/or relevant, be supported by either an invoice or detailed estimate.

4.5 All aspects of the claim including the VAT status of the landlord, if appropriate, should be set out.

4.6 If the claim includes any other losses for example, (a) surveyor's fees for preparing the schedule; (b) professional or other fees or expenses incurred or to be incurred in connection with the carrying out of the remedial works (c) preliminaries; and (d) loss of rent, service charge or insurance rent, these must be set out in detail substantiated and fully quantified. The landlord should also explain the legal basis for any such claim i.e. whether it is made as part of the damages claim or under some express or implied provision of the lease.

4.7 The claim should generally contain the following information:

- the landlord's full name and address;
- the tenant's full name and address;
- a clear summary of the facts on which the claim is based;
- the schedule referred to above;
- a clear summary of the monetary sums the landlord is claiming as damages in respect of the breaches. This may include the cost of the works, the consequential costs and fees, VAT, loss of rent and other losses (including any sums paid to a superior landlord);
- any documents relied upon or required by this protocol, including copies of any receipted invoices or other evidence of such costs and losses;

- confirmation that the landlord and/or its professional advisers will attend a meeting or meetings as proposed under section 7 below;
- a date (being a reasonable time) by which the tenant should respond. In the usual case 56 days should be adopted as a reasonable time.

4.8   Assessment of Loss

4.8.1   The landlord's claim should be restricted to its loss. This is not necessarily the same as the cost of works to remedy the breaches.

4.8.2   The claim should not include any items likely to be superseded by works to be carried out by the landlord or items likely to be superseded by the landlord's intentions for the property.

4.8.3   The claim must contain a written endorsement by the surveyor(s) preparing it that the overall figure claimed is a fair assessment of the landlord's loss.

4.8.4   In making this assessment the surveyor(s) should have regard to the principles laid down in the Royal Institution of Chartered Surveyors' Guidance Note on Dilapidations, the common law principles of how that loss should be calculated and, in relation to repairing covenants, s18(1) of the Landlord and Tenant Act 1927 ("s18(1)"). (Appendix B)

4.8.5   A formal quantification of the landlord's loss based on either a formal diminution valuation or an account of the actual expenditure or a combination of both must be provided by the landlord to the tenant prior to issuing proceedings. (See section 10 below.)

5. The Response

5.1   The tenant must respond to the claim within a reasonable time. In the usual case 56 days should be adopted as a reasonable time.

5.2   The tenant should respond using the schedule provided by the landlord, where appropriate, in sufficient detail to enable the landlord to understand clearly the tenant's views on each item of claim.

5.3   If the tenant considers that any items in the claim are likely to be superseded by works to be carried out by the landlord or items likely to be superseded by the landlord's intentions for the property he should state this in his response and should give particulars of that on which he relies e.g. correspondence or minutes of the landlord company (see 6 below), and he should also state the items in the landlord's claim to which this contention is relevant.

6. Disclosure of Documents

Disclosure will generally be limited to the documents required to be enclosed with the claim letter and the tenant's response. The parties can agree that further disclosure may be given. If either or both of the parties consider that further disclosure should be given but there is disagreement about some aspect of that process, they may be able to make an application for pre-action disclosure under CPR Part 31.

7. Negotiations

7.1 The landlord and tenant and/or their respective professional advisers are encouraged to meet before the tenant is required to respond to the claim and must generally meet within 28 days of service of the tenant's response. The meetings will be without prejudice and preferably on site, to review the schedule to ensure that the tenant understands fully all aspects of the landlord's claim and the parties should seek to agree as many of the items in dispute as possible.

7.2 In a complex matter it may be necessary for more than one site visit or without prejudice meeting between the parties to take place. These ought to be conducted without unnecessary delay.

8. Alternative Dispute Resolution

8.1 The parties should consider whether some form of alternative dispute resolution procedure would be more suitable than litigation, and if so, endeavour to agree which form to adopt. Both the landlord and tenant may be required by the Court to provide evidence that alternative means of resolving their dispute were considered. The Courts take the view that litigation should be a last resort, and that claims should not be issued prematurely when a settlement is still actively being explored. Parties are warned that if the protocol is not followed (including this paragraph) then the Court must have regard to such conduct when determining costs.

8.2 It is not practicable in this protocol to address in detail how the parties might decide which method to adopt to resolve their particular dispute. However, summarised below are some of the options for resolving disputes without litigation:

- Discussion and negotiation.
- Early neutral evaluation by an independent third party (for example, a lawyer experienced in that field or an individual experienced in the subject matter of the claim).
- Mediation—a form of facilitated negotiation assisted by an independent neutral party.

The Legal Services Commission has published a booklet on "Alternatives to Court", CLS Direct Information Leaflet 23 (www.clsdirect.org.uk/legal help/leaflet23.jsp), which lists a number of organisations that provide alternative dispute resolution services.

It is expressly recognised that no party can or should be forced to mediate or enter into any form of ADR.

9. Stocktake

Where a claim is not resolved when the protocol has been followed, the parties might wish to carry out a "stocktake" of the issues in dispute, and the evidence (including technical evidence) that the court is likely to need to decide those issues, before proceedings are started.

10. Formal Diminution Valuation and Quantification of the Claim prior to Issue of Proceedings (NB See flowchart at Annex C)

10.1.1 Any technical evidence which might be presented to the Court should be prepared in an appropriate manner by an appropriately qualified

Expert. Attention is drawn to Civil Procedure Rules rule 35.4(1) 'No party may call an expert or put in evidence an expert's report without the Court's permission. Protocol for the Instruction of Experts to give Evidence in Civil Claims: http://www.dca.gov.uk/civil/procrules_fin/contents/form_section_nimages/practice_directions/pd35_pdf_eps/pd35_prot.pdf

10.1.2   The landlord must quantify its loss by providing to the tenant a detailed breakdown of the issues and consequential losses based on either a formal diminution valuation or an account of the actual expenditure or a combination of both. For these purposes a formal diminution valuation is a valuation showing the diminution in value to the landlord's reversionary interest in the property due to the fact that the tenant has not complied with its covenants or obligations relating to the physical state of the property.

10.1.3   If a formal diminution valuation is produced it should be prepared by a valuer. Only one valuation is required which takes account of both s18(1) in relation to breaches of covenants or obligations to repair, and common law principles of loss for other covenants or obligations.

10.2.1   If the landlord has carried out the work it considers should have been done to remedy the breaches of covenant or obligations, it is not usually required to provide a formal diminution valuation but may base the claim on an account of the actual expenditure. However, the landlord should provide a formal diminution valuation if in all the circumstances it would be reasonable to do so.

10.2.2   If the landlord has carried out some of the work but not all of it, it is not usually required to provide a formal diminution valuation in relation to the work which has been done but may base the claim for those works on an account of the actual expenditure. However, the landlord should provide a formal diminution valuation if in all the circumstances it would be reasonable to do so. With regard to the remaining works it should comply as in 10.2.3 or 10.2.4 below depending on whether or not it intends to carry out those remaining works.

10.2.3   If the landlord has not carried out the work but intends to, it must state when it intends to do the work, and what steps it has taken towards getting the work done, e.g. preparing a specification or bills of quantities or inviting tenders. The scope of the landlord's proposed works should be clearly shown to enable any effect on the dilapidations claim to be identified. The landlord should provide a formal diminution valuation unless, in all the circumstances, it would be reasonable not to.

10.2.4   If the landlord does not intend to carry out the work, then it should provide a formal diminution valuation for comparison with the schedule based claim in order to establish whether the claim is capped by the valuation unless, in all the circumstances, it would be reasonable not to.

10.3   If the tenant relies on a defence on the basis of diminution, it must state its case for so doing and provide a diminution valuation to the landlord. If a formal diminution valuation is produced only one valuation is required which takes account of both s18(1) in relation to breaches of covenants or obligations to repair, and common law principles of loss for other covenants or obligations.

10.4   The tenant's diminution valuation shall be served within a reasonable time. A "reasonable time" will vary from case to case but generally will not be more than 56 days after the landlord has served his quantified claim under 10.1.2.

11. Court Proceedings

If the parties cannot reach a settlement after complying with the protocol then the final step will be for the dispute to be referred to the Court.

ANNEX A

SCHEDULE OF DILAPIDATIONS

This schedule has been prepared by [name, individual and firm], upon the instructions of [name the landlord]. It was prepared following [name i.e. same name as above]'s inspection of the property known as [property] on [date].

It records the works required to be done to the property in order that they are put into the physical state the property should have been put if the tenant [name] had complied with its covenants or obligations contained within its lease of the property dated [   ].

The covenants of the said lease with which the tenant should have complied are as follows:-

[Set out clause number of the lease and quote the clause verbatim].

The following schedule contains:
- reference to the specific clause (quoted above) under which the obligation arises,
- the breach complained of,
- the remedial works suggested by the landlord's surveyor [name i.e. same name as above] as suitable for remedying the breach complained of,
- the landlord's view on the cost of the works.

The schedule contains the true views of [name, i.e. the same name as above] being the surveyor appointed/employed by the landlord to prepare the schedule.

Upon receipt of this schedule the tenant should respond using this schedule in the relevant column below to enable the landlord to understand clearly the tenant's views on each item of claim.

1	2	3	4	5
Item No.	Clause No.	Breach complained of	Remedial works required	Landlord's costings

DATED [.......................]

SIGNED [.......................]

[Name and address of surveyor appointed by landlord]

ANNEX B

SECTION 18(1) OF THE LANDLORD AND TENANT ACT 1927

Provisions as to covenants to repair

Damages for a breach of a covenant or agreement to keep or put premises in repair during the currency of a lease, or to leave or put premises in repair at the termination of a lease, whether such covenant or agreement is expressed or implied, and whether general or specific, shall in no case exceed the amount (if any) by which the value of the reversion (whether immediate or not) in the premises is diminished owing to the breach of such covenant or agreement as aforesaid; and in particular no damage shall be recovered for a breach of any such covenant or agreement to leave or put premises in repair at the termination of a lease, if it is shown that the premises, in whatever state of repair they might be, would at or shortly after the termination of the tenancy have been or be pulled down, or such structural alterations made therein as would render valueless the repairs covered by the covenant or agreement.

ANNEX C

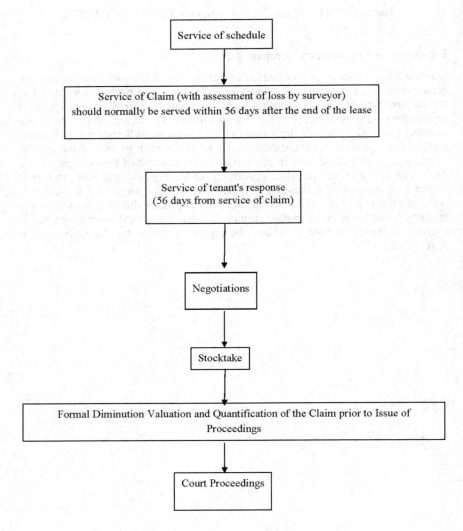

NB:
1. The parties should consider throughout this process whether ADR would assist in settling the dispute.

2. Service in this context means the issuing of the relevant document to the tenant or landlord by the other party, its surveyor or solicitor as appropriate, and should be in accordance with any provisions laid down in the lease as to service.

INDEX